JAZZ ÉTUDES
STUDIES FOR THE BEGINNING IMPROVISER

By Joshua Breakstone

Cover art by Levin Pfeufer

Back cover photo by Michael G. Stewart
www.michaelgstewart.com

Photo on page 5 by Al Sachs

Recording Credits: Joshua Breakstone, Guitar

Cherry Lane Music Company
Educational Director/Project Supervisor: Susan Poliniak
Director of Publications: Mark Phillips
Publications Coordinator: Rebecca Skidmore

ISBN 978-1-60378-060-5

Visit our website at www.cherrylaneprint.com

CONTENTS

INTRODUCTION

This is a collection of jazz études for the beginning improviser. Each étude is an improvisation of one or more choruses based on the chord progression of a well-known jazz standard. My hope is that you'll know many of the progressions upon which these études are based. In all cases, it would be a great study not only to be able to play these études fluently, but also to learn the standards that serve as their bases.

Each étude is written with virtually all notes to be found within the position indicated at the start of the piece (there's more on the concept of position in *A Simple Guide to Signs and Notation*). In the few cases where notes fall outside the indicated position, the way of playing these notes (fingering and position) has been clearly notated and often described in the accompanying notes (*Hands On!*).

The instruments we play—whether they are guitars, basses, saxophones, whatever—are all extensions of the instrument that each one of us possesses and with which we express ourselves so naturally and instinctively, that each of us uses in our own unique and individual way: our voice. Learn to play these études smoothly and beautifully—just the way you would sing them.

A very brief note on chord playing: When we first learn how to *comp,* or play a chordal accompaniment, we normally play a basic and rather generic form of the written chord symbol indicated. With experience, however, we come to understand that when playing chords, we need to be aware of the melody. In this way, we can play notes that work with what is being played melodically, rather than create clashes. We as guitarists also need to be aware of the rhythm of the melody—again, so you can play something that works, but here in a rhythmic sense. Remember this as you navigate your way through this book and try to bring an increased awareness of melody, harmony, and rhythm into your chord playing.

I have not indicated any picking in this book (other than in the *Hands On!* guides to several of the études), and yet I would like to touch on this very important subject. I am a definite proponent of *alternate picking,* which does not mean merely alternating downstrokes and upstrokes. What alternate picking *does* mean is the playing of all downbeats (the 1s, 2s, 3s, and 4s) with downstrokes, and all upbeats (the "ands") with upstrokes. Why? We guitar players don't have the same bodily connection to our instruments as horn players, who blow into their instruments. Alternate picking puts us in touch with our natural body movement by having us pick down when our bodies feel like moving down and having us pick up when our bodies feel like moving up. The simplest guide to this is to watch your foot tapping time—on all of the downbeats, your foot goes down, and it comes back up on all the "ands"—which is the perfect embodiment of the principle of alternate picking. So, we pick in coordination with our bodies, naturally. All of this is covered in greater depth in *A Simple Guide to Alternate Picking.*

I've mentioned the voice. Isn't it amazing that every one of us has our own unique way of speaking? Let's briefly consider the few expressive devices that each one of us uses all of the time—without having been taught—and that make our speech so personal and individually communicative, full of nuance and meaning. These devices include the direction of lines (whether the things we say move up or down in pitch), the use of faster pitches (pitches of shorter duration) versus slower pitches (pitches of longer duration), the use of space (the presence or absence of sound), and the relative increase or decrease in volume. The use and, even more important, the balancing of these dynamics, when applied to the music we play, can make our playing more expressive, unique, and personal. No two people use these dynamics in the same way. Never lose sight of the fact that this is our goal in playing music: to develop our own voice, our own way of communicating something special, something personal, and something unique. More on the use of the dynamics of vocal expression to come!

This book can benefit your ability to read in various positions all over the guitar. I hope it will also be of use to you in learning how to improvise over jazz harmonies, and in the process of developing your own unique and special voice as an improviser and musician.

ABOUT THE AUTHOR

"Fire in velvet. A fitting description of Joshua Breakstone's jazz guitar," wrote Paul Weidman in *The Sante Fe New Mexican.* "His flowing lines on up-tempo cookers are impeccably clean and fiery, bearing the mark of a first-rate improviser, while his chordal work on heartbreaker ballads is the final word in finesse," has raved *Guitar Player* magazine. Japan's *Jazz Hihyo* (A.K.A. *Jazz Critique*) recognizes that "The style in which Joshua develops his fluid single-note solos used to be thought of as the Grant Green school, but now this man leads the school." *Downbeat* also has written "There is no shortage of young, knock-out jazz guitarists about us these days. And Joshua Breakstone is among the best of them."

Joshua Breakstone was born July 22, 1955, in Elizabeth, NJ. He studied with guitar great Sal Salvador, whom he describes as "a great person, teacher, guitarist, and also a great friend. Sal exposed me to a broad range of music and helped me accomplish a lot on the instrument in a relatively short time." Joshua graduated from New College of the University of South Florida (including two terms at Berklee College of Music in Boston) in 1975.

He began his recording career in 1989 and has recorded 19 CDs to date as a leader alongside such jazz greats as Barry Harris, Kenny Barron, Tommy Flanagan, Jack McDuff, Jimmy Knepper, Pepper Adams, Kenny Washington, Mickey Roker, Al Harewood, Ray Drummond, and Dennis Irwin.

"In teaching, either in clinics or individually, I describe to students the progression we make as jazz musicians, beginning with learning to improvise, to melodically negotiate any harmonic terrain—which could be a lifetime of work right there. But when we take a step back, it becomes clear that to have become an improviser is not really to have accomplished anything at all—for the ultimate goal in jazz is self-expression, not just to be able to improvise, but to have a unique voice, to say something in one's own way. It's only in taking this leap—from being an improviser to becoming a communicator—that we go from the level of craftsman (in the sense of having mastered the craft of improvisation, being able to spontaneously play melodies over harmony) to becoming an artist. As for myself, my idea has always been to try and say something straight from my heart. It's always been my conviction that if you express something unique, in your own way and honestly in your music, there will always be an audience there for you, that you'll always be all right."

For additional information on Joshua's performing, recording, and teaching careers, for private instruction, or to contact Joshua directly, go to Joshua's website, www.joshuabreakstone.com.

Note: Track 1 contains tuning pitches.

(♪♪ = ♪♪) All music examples are played in a swing rhythm unless otherwise noted.

TRACK 01

A SIMPLE GUIDE TO ALTERNATE PICKING

Here's the rundown on picking. As guitar players, we don't have the same physical connection to our instruments as wind players—we don't rely on our breath for phrasing. However, through the practice of alternate picking, we can make up for this deficit and play in coordination with the natural feel and movement of our bodies.

Alternate picking does NOT mean continually playing down-up-down-up, etc.

What it *does* mean is that all the 1s, 2s, 3s, and 4s of a measure—also known as the *downbeats*—are played with a downstroke. All of the "ands" (or *upbeats*, the eighth notes immediately after each downbeat) are played with an upstroke.

Why? How does following this picking get us in sync with our bodies?

Below, you'll see two measures of 4/4 time, which consist solely of quarter notes (one note per beat). Each measure is counted 1–2–3–4, and therefore picked entirely with downstrokes. (By the way, notice in the music below the symbol for a downstroke—a sort of bracket on its side—is above each note.) If you tap your foot in time with the example below you'll notice that your foot moves down with the playing of each quarter note. In other words, your body moves in the same direction as your guitar pick.

Below, you'll find two measures of 4/4 that consist solely of eighth notes. Now, the beat is divided into two halves (two eighth notes per beat). And the count goes 1–and–2–and–3–and–4–and. Therefore, pick with alternate downstrokes and upstrokes. If you tap your foot in time with the music below, you will notice that your foot moves down on each downbeat and comes back up on each upbeat. In other words, your body moves in the same way as your guitar pick.

This is the essence of alternate picking.

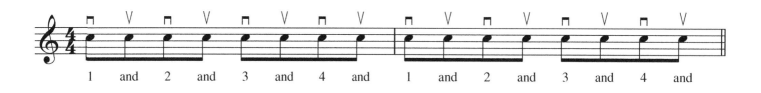

In playing eighth notes and longer durations, all measures are counted 1–and–2–and–3–and–4–and. How those notes are arranged is what determines the picking, but essentially it is a simple matter. As stated above, all downbeats are played with a downstroke and all upbeats are played with an upstroke.

The four music examples below consist of eighth notes combined with quarter notes. (There are some ties and a half note thrown in for good measure!) Some of the articulations fall on the downbeats, while others are on *offbeats* (another word for upbeats, or the "ands"). Remember what we said above: Determining the correct picking is dependent on how the rhythmic values (durations) of the notes in each measure are arranged. To clarify the duration of each note, I've added parentheses.

To practice your picking, try repeating each of these examples until you can play them easily, with your pick moving in coordination with your foot. If you find that counting out loud helps you to identify where the upstrokes and downstrokes fall, then use this device in the beginning until you really *know*.

Don't worry. All of this will start coming naturally soon.

Below are some examples of rhythms. Can you count the beats and determine the proper picking? The answers are at the back of the book on page 62. Each of the following examples should be repeated until the picking becomes clear and second nature.

A SIMPLE GUIDE TO SIGNS AND NOTATION

I've written this section in order to clarify and simplify some of the notation that you will see throughout this book.

All notation, be it general music notation or notation specific to the guitar, boils down to signs. These signs give you information; they tell you what to do.

For us as guitarists, the first bit of notation we encounter when we pick up a piece of music is the *G clef* (also known as the *treble clef*). Sure, it looks great, but what is its purpose? It's a sign and gives us some vital information without which we'd be unable to proceed at all. Very simply, it shows us (by wrapping around the second line of the staff) where to find the note G.

And once we know where G is, we know where all of the other notes can be found.

These notes can be extended by the addition of *ledger lines*—little lines that can be written in, as needed, either above or below the staff.

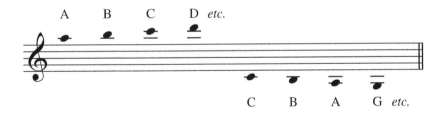

Next to the G clef there's another sign: the *key signature*. Since every key, major and minor, has its own unique number of either flats or sharps, the key signature is essential information. In the case of the one here, it can indicate the key of A♭ major or F minor. Keep in mind that key signatures can change within the course of a piece of music. In *Étude 11*, for example, you'll find that the key changes four times in just 48 measures. Whoa, good luck!

Next, there's the *time signature*. The top number indicates how many beats there are per measure. The bottom number indicates what kind of note gets one beat, For example, if the lower number is four, the quarter note gets one beat; if the bottom number is eight, the eighth note gets one beat; if the bottom number is two, the half note gets one beat, etc.

For instance, in 3/4, there are three beats per measure, and the quarter note gets one beat.

In 5/4, there are five beats per measure, and the quarter note gets one beat.

In 7/8, there are seven beats per measure, and the eighth note gets one beat.

In 2/2, there are two beats per measure, and the half note gets one beat.

Now that we've briefly covered the G clef, key signatures, and time signatures, let's look at notation that is specific to the guitar. This is notation that you'll be seeing a lot throughout this book.

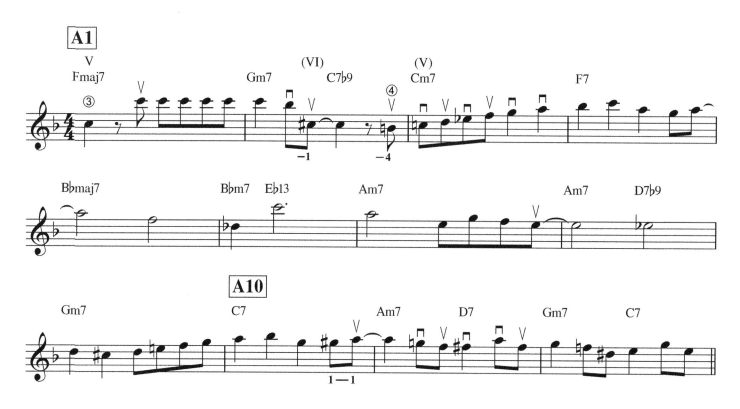

The first thing you may notice is the Roman numeral at the start of each étude. In the case of the music example above, it's a "V." This Roman numeral indicates the *position*. What's a position? The position defines where on the neck of the guitar a song or passage should be played. But why should we need to indicate where to play things? This is because, in many cases, the same notes can be played in several different places. If you want to show someone (perhaps as a composer or teacher) where you'd like a song or passage played, or even if you'd like to mark it down for yourself in the process of composing, rehearsing, or learning to play a piece of music, you'll want to indicate a position.

The position indicates where (i.e., at which fret) the 1st finger goes. In the case of the piece above, *Étude 7*, it is the 5th fret. Keep this in mind: The position marking tells you only where to put your hand, but not which string to play, nor which finger to use to fret a note. There is other notation to indicate strings and fingers, and we'll cover that next.

Knowing where on the neck to play is vital, but the implications of hand position are also important. Using the excerpt from *Étude 7* as an example, it seems obvious that if the 1st finger lies on the 5th fret, then the 2nd finger should play the notes on the 6th fret (on any string), the 3rd finger should take the notes on the 7th fret, and the 4th finger should take those on the 8th fret. Knowing this, you can maintain a hand position where each finger lies directly above its designated space. You'll hardly have to look to see where you are if you maintain a good hand position. However, many times you will need to play notes outside the range of the position you're in (such as in measures 2 and 10). What then? More on that coming up, I promise!

The next notational device you may notice in scanning across the music is the "3" in a circle (and in the following measure, a circled "4" as well). This is how strings are indicated, and they are normally notated above the staff.

Now, we get to fingers and fingering, which are often accompanied by dashes. Dashes can mean two things. First, as you can see at A2, a dash can mean that a fret has been skipped. In the case of "-1," the 1st finger is playing at the 6th fret rather than at its usual V-position spot, at the 5th fret. The last note of that same measure also falls outside of the normal V position—the 4th finger skips to the 9th fret to play a B♮. This is one of the two ways a dash is used with respect to fingerings. What's the other way? Read on!

An example of the other use of a dash in fingering notation can be found at A10. In this case the dash indicates a *slide*, with the same finger being used twice. It's important to keep in mind that even though you are sliding the finger, the slide should not be in any way audible or detectable—both notes should receive their full values in terms of time and sound.

Finally, there's picking. Picking is an essential part of playing well, and therefore it's important to see where downstrokes and upstrokes are indicated. In the first measure, you can see the upstroke sign (the "V"-shaped figure) indicated on the first of the five C eighth notes (on the "and" of beat 2). At A2 you can see the downstroke on the B♭ (beat 2) followed by the upstroke on the C♯ (which falls on the next eighth note). For much more on alternate picking, refer to *A Simple Guide to Alternate Picking*.

Remember my promise to say a little more about the playing of notes that fall outside a position? Don't say I ever reneged on a promise!

There are two basic hand positions, *closed* and *open*, and it's a really simple matter to go from one to the other—it's just a matter of opening up your hand a little (as opposed to keeping each finger directly above its designated fret, as described above). So, in the case of the B♮ at A2, played with the 4th finger on the 9th fret (one fret above where that finger normally plays in V position), you should play this note by opening your hand while keeping your other fingers in roughly the same places they would normally lie in the V position. Don't move your entire hand up to play, as doing so would necessitate moving the hand back again in order to play the following note—too much movement. Opening and closing the hand is simpler and, especially as you progress to play at quicker tempos, more efficient.

By the way, in this book you won't find many notes that fall outside the position indicated at the beginning of an étude.

ÉTUDE 1

TRACK 02

HANDS ON!

We took a look at how to approach alternate picking in the *Simple Guide to Alternate Picking*. In the études, however, we'll be working not only with rhythms but with notes as well. Keep in mind that you can approach any challenging sections exactly as you did with the rhythmic examples in the introduction—by isolating the measures in question, by defining the division of time, and by repeating the section in question until the picking becomes easy and second nature, as in the first two measures below.

Melodically, measures 1 and 2 are very close to the well-known standard upon which this étude is based. (Another snippet of that same melody pops up again at B5!) Alteration of the original melody of a song, varying it rhythmically or melodically, is probably the simplest and most basic but also, in many ways, the strongest route one can take with regard to melodic improvisation.

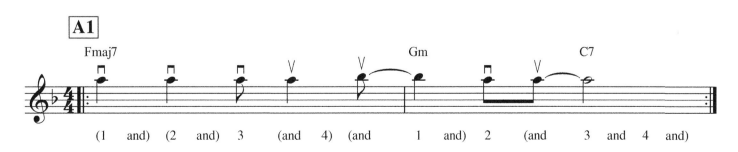

Note that measures 9, 10, and 11 are composed entirely of only two notes, altered rhythmically, which then lead naturally to measures 12 and beyond. Remember that it's not always what you play that is of paramount importance, but what you do with the material you play.

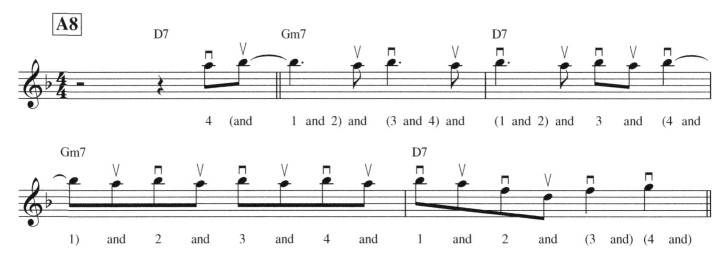

Take note that the first two measures of this eight-measure section are almost identical rhythmically to what follows in A21 and 22. Again, it's not always what you play, but what you do with the things you play. Here is an example of material being developed rhythmically and then leading us naturally to the next idea. It's great to have some notes of longer duration after all of the eighth notes that preceded, don't you think? Balance! (Also see measures A25, 29, etc., and measures B17–18 and B25–27.)

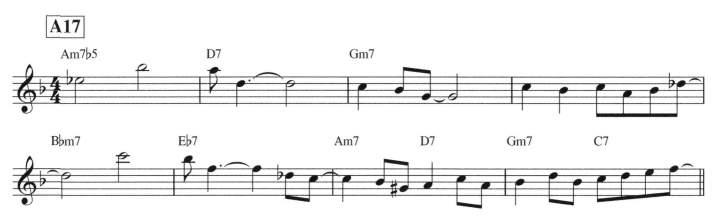

Here, we find references to the melodies of two well-known songs. Considering that improvisation is the spontaneous creation of new melodies, it should come as no surprise that in jazz, references to melodic material other than that of the song on which we're improvising is pretty common.

At B19 there are three measures of rhythmic development. The rhythmic motif is a quarter note followed by two eighth notes, tied to a quarter note followed by two eighth notes, etc. This motif leads naturally into something new: in this case, the quarter notes of B22–24. (Note the development of the rhythm in B22 by its return in B24.) The rhythms of B19–21 are balanced by the whole notes of B17–18 and the predominant quarter notes of B22–24.

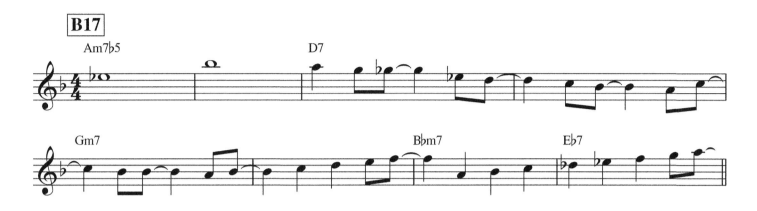

At B31, begin the frequently used ending (or tag) iii–VI–ii–V, by going not to the I chord as expected, but by substituting the iii chord (in this case the chord has been altered by adding the ♭5) for the I chord. This tag (B31–34), although it appears here only once, can be repeated as many times as you like until it finally ends by resolving on the final I chord.

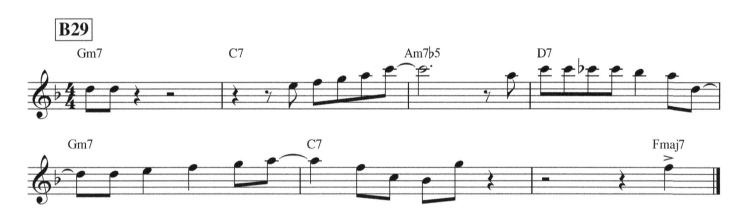

A Note on the Subject of Interpretation

Although for the most part the recorded examples have been played as written, you'll notice that here and there I couldn't resist taking liberties by adding some expressive elements (such as hammer-ons, pull-offs, etc.) that are not notated. I encourage you to make these études "your own" as much as possible: Think about subtly slowing down or speeding up in places, and consider bringing out passages by increasing or decreasing in volume. I hope the playing of these études will be of benefit to you in your continuing development as an improviser. But to take that next step—from learning to improvise to developing your own expressive voice—it's not just a question of what you play, but of how you play whatever it is you are playing. I encourage you to play these études as expressively as possible and in your own way.

ÉTUDE 2

TRACK 03

HANDS ON!

Let's start by taking a more in-depth look at the first two measures of *Étude 2*.

When in doubt (or just for practice), we can always isolate the picking by playing the rhythm on just one note as below, and repeating it until it's really comfortable.

You can extend (or develop) rhythms as well, continuing them over greater lengths of time, over a section of a song, or even over an entire chorus of a song. But more on that later (particularly in the *Hands On!* commentary for Études 3, 5, and 11).

This rhythm, which is repeated in the first two measures, gives rise to the rhythm of the third, fourth, and fifth measures (and beyond). Let's take a quick look.

Isolating the picking . . .

Now let's go from rhythm and picking and turn our attention to harmony. If you take a look at the third measure below (A7), you'll see the G7 chord—the tonic chord of our blues in G—that moves to the E7. The E7 serves to move us to the chord that follows at measure A9, the A7 chord.

Let's take a look at the same place in Chorus 2—at measure B7—where there's a chromatic bridge between the G7 chord and the E7 chord by adding the Gb7♯5 and the F13 chords.

Moving forward to Chorus 3—at measure C7—you'll see another slightly different treatment at the same place in this blues harmony. This is a kind of "middle ground," where the G7 tonic moves to the F7, which then leads to the E7.

Harmonic motion is the term that describes the frequency of the change in harmony. In other words, it's the rate at which the chords change, whether over an entire song, or just over the course of a few measures. In the first of the three examples we've just looked at (in Chorus 1), there is the slowest harmonic rhythm, only one chord per measure. The example taken from Chorus 2, where the chords change every two beats, has the quickest. The above, from Chorus 3, takes the middle ground. It's not a really big deal, but sometimes it's nice to be able to add chords—to increase the harmonic rhythm—in order to add interest and movement. To do so requires some experience and some knowledge of harmony. It's definitely something to consider!

Let's consider fingerings for a minute. Why? Because using the simplest fingerings with the least amount of extraneous movement will serve you well—it's actually essential—as the demands of the music you play become increasingly more challenging both melodically, as well as in terms of tempo.

Let's take a look at measures B4–5, and also at measures B6–7.

In the III position, the G, E, and C of measures B4 and B5 would all normally be played with the 3rd finger. So playing these three notes in succession would entail either laying the 3rd finger down or rocking the 3rd finger along the 5th fret—not so easy, particularly at a quicker tempo. What to do? Let's take a look at a few possibilities. Don't be scared, this looks complicated, but it's actually pretty simple.

Fingering option #1: Play the G with the 3rd finger (where it normally lies in the III position), and follow with the 4th finger (on the fret where the 3rd finger would normally play), which is free and therefore available. To play the C, rock between strings with the 4th finger.

Fingering option #2: As with #1, play the G with the 3rd finger (where it normally lies) and follow with the 4th finger (on the fret where the 3rd finger would normally play), which is free and therefore available. But then, to play the C, go back to the 3rd finger. Note that #2 and #5 are the only ones out of the five fingerings that don't require a rocking motion of a finger (either the 3rd or 4th) between neighboring strings.

Fingering #3: Play the G not with the 3rd finger (where it would normally lie), but with the 2nd finger, which skips a fret to play a fret above where it would normally lie. Follow with the available 3rd finger, and then to play the C, rock between strings, and rock back with the 3rd finger to play the E that follows.

Fingering #4: As with #3, play the G not with the 3rd finger (where it would normally lie), but with the 2nd finger, which skips a fret to play a fret above where it would normally lie. Follow with the available 3rd finger and then to play the C, rock between strings. However, to play the E, go to the available 4th finger.

Fingering #5: As with #3, play the G not with the 3rd finger (where it would normally lie), but with the 2nd finger, which skips a fret to play a fret above where it would normally lie. Follow with the available 3rd finger, and then to play the C, go back again to the 2nd finger. To play the E, go back to the 3rd finger.

OK, so after all of this discussion and our brief look at five (!) different fingerings, which is the best? What do you think? You probably suspect that I'm about to give you my own ideas on the subject and, if so, you're right. The best fingering, in my own opinion, in any situation, is always the one that is most comfortable for you. But remember—everything you play should be evaluated by the application of the most fundamental and yet basic of questions: How do the things we play sound? I've had students who play passages such as this one by rocking the fingers, and every note is beautiful, clear, and legato. If so, fine. The way to judge the right or wrong of anything you play is, in the final analysis, by the sound of what it is you're playing. But I'll add this: For me, personally, fingerings #2 and #5 are the way to go—no rocking, efficient, simple. Thanks for bearing with me through this slightly complicated jungle of fingerings. More on this subject to come!

ÉTUDE 3

TRACK 04

HANDS ON!

Since we encounter the same rhythm three times in this eight-measure section—a half note, followed by a dotted quarter note, followed by an eighth note that is tied over to the next measure—let's take a closer look at the picking of this rhythm.

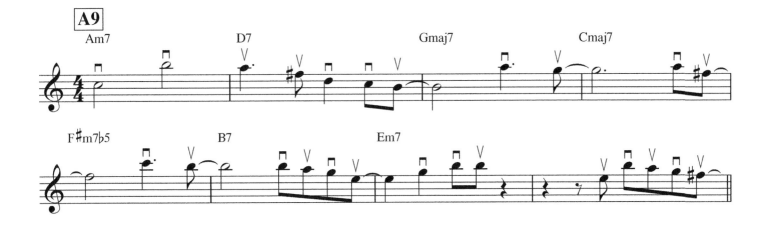

It's a great exercise to be able to improvise over a song, confining yourself to just one rhythm. If you can do this, you really have control over what you are playing! What do I mean? Let's take a look at the section above and—just for fun—let's see what would happen if we were to limit ourselves to only one rhythm.

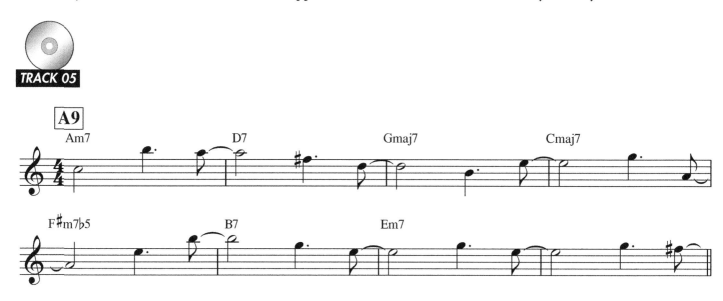

C'mon, let's try it again. Let's see what would happen if we confine ourselves to just one rhythm over a section of the étude. At A25 we find several measures of half notes . . .

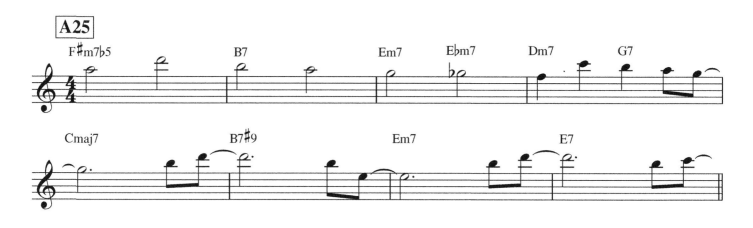

. . . so let's try continuing them.

Try this yourself. Limit yourself to one rhythm, just as you did in the above two examples, for either a section of a song or for an entire form! Take one of the rhythms above, or come up with one on your own.

The last measures of Chorus 1 give rise to the new material found here in the first four measures of Chorus 2. These four measures lead, in turn, to measures 5–7 where the same melody is repeated, but this time against a different harmonic backdrop—that of E minor. At measure B8 you can see that the harmony changes from Em7 to E7, and the melody outlines that change with the addition of the G♯, the major 3rd of the chord.

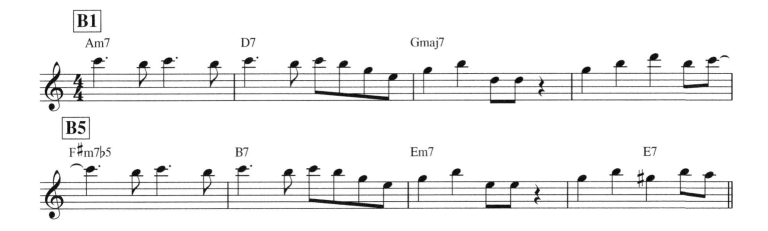

Measure B8 of Chorus 2 serves to lead us to the new ideas of B9–12, an example of playing a phrase consisting of an odd number of beats—in this case, three—and repeating it against the pulse of four beats per measure. It's a great rhythmic effect.

Starting at B31 and continuing for four measures to B34, you'll find another idea for an ending (or *tag*), other than the so-often-played iii–VI–ii–V (see the end of *Étude 1*). As is true of the iii–VI–ii–V, this "bluesy" ending can be extended by repeating it over and over as many times as you like. Then you can resolve it on the final chord—in this case, Em9.

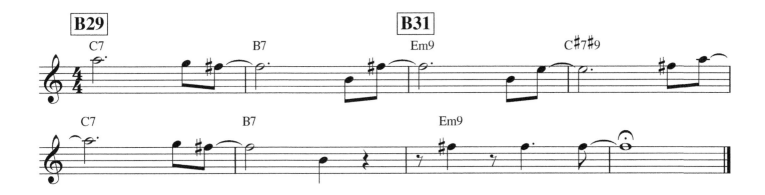

ÉTUDE 4

TRACK 07

♩ = 122

A1

HANDS ON!

The first thing you should do when you have a piece of music dropped down in front of you at a rehearsal, a performance, a recording date, etc., is to take a look at it—to scan it. You don't need to be able to sight-sing to look at a piece of music and get a pretty good idea of what's going on. First, identify the key and time signature. Then, check out the *range*. Is the music very high, very low, or in a middle range (are most of the notes above, below, or on the staff)? In the case of the études you'll find in this book, the *position*—or place on the neck where the piece is to be played—is indicated. But in real life, you'll want to scan the music so as to get a feel for which position(s) might be the best in which to play the piece.

In scanning the music—even very briefly—you can get an idea of what's happening in a given piece. In the case of *Étude 4*, it jumps out that there are notes of long duration running through the first eight measures, followed by mostly eighth notes in the following eight. This general pattern recurs throughout the entire piece. Now, you are not only mentally prepared for what's to come, but you also can appreciate the rhythmic balance in the piece—one of the essential elements of this étude.

In a sight-reading situation, after having scanned the piece in a general way as described above, then you can, as much as time allows, direct your attention to spots that might be especially difficult, due either to range (very low or very high passages), speed (16th notes, etc.), syncopation, and many other things.

For the melodies you play to be as expressive as possible, you need to be aware of and to be able to use the dynamics of expression we touched on in the introduction.

How about the use of tensions and dissonance (as opposed to the use of scale or chord tones)?

It's easy to see that *Étude 4* is composed almost exclusively of either the strong tones of chords—the roots, 3rds, and 5ths—or notes that move along the scale. One exception is to be found at B8. Let's take a look.

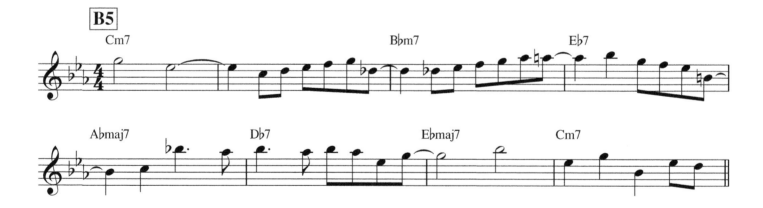

At B8, an A♮ (the ♭5th of the E♭7 chord) is carried over from the preceding measure—definitely not a chord tone. The A♮ resolves to the B♭. Shortly thereafter, there's a B♮ (the last note of B8) that carries over against the A♭maj7 at B9—again, definitely not a chord tone (it's the minor 3rd of the chord). The B♮ resolves to the C.

Here, the melody has been made more dynamic—more interesting, more expressive—by contrasting the consonant chord and scale tones with a bit of dissonance. Just for fun, let's continue our use of dissonance beyond B9.

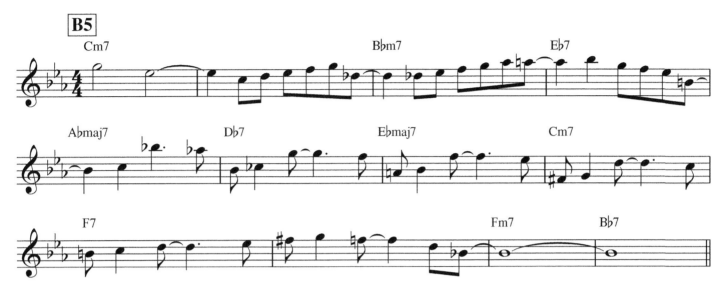

In this example, you can see the use of the ♭5 (the G) at B10, and then the resolution of the ♭5s at B11, 12, and 13. At B14 there's a ♭9. This is by no means earth-shattering, but it's certainly different harmonically from what came before—and, in the case of the example above, the use of tensions (and their resolutions) is then developed over the course of several measures.

Here's another example of the same idea, the use and subsequent resolution of dissonance.

Once again, the use of stable chord tones or notes of the scale balanced against the use of dissonant notes that want to resolve back to more stable chord tones is a dynamic you should be familiar with, and be able to use to add an extra element of expressiveness to your playing.

ÉTUDE 5

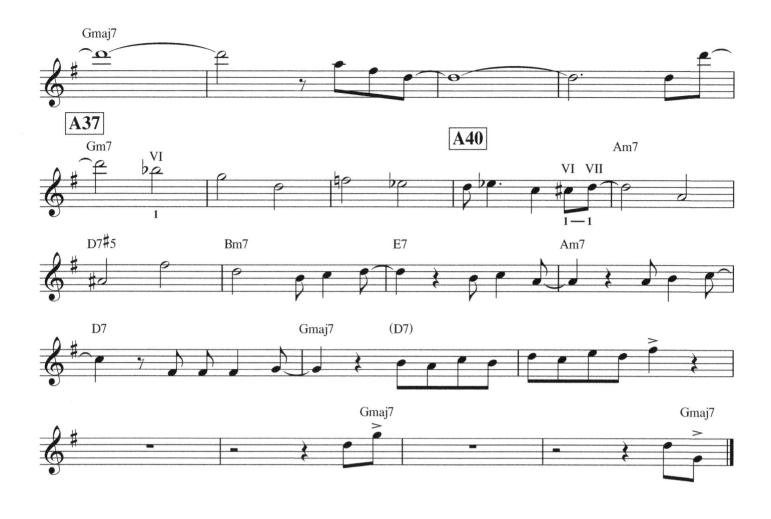

HANDS ON!

In the first 12 measures of this étude, you can see illustrated in a very simple way three important principles of improvisation: outlining the chords in a melody, maintaining a balance in the duration of notes, and rhythmic development.

Outlining of the Chords in the Melody

In the first four measures you have a G major triad—against the Gmaj7 chord—that then leads by a series of notes that move in steps along the G major scale to a G minor triad (A5–8) against the Gm7 chord. The melody of the first four measures is repeated in the next four with only one change: Whereas the Gmaj7 of the first four measures demands a B♮ (the major 3rd of the chord), the Gm7 of the next four measures requires a B♭ (the lowered or minor 3rd). Notice that the B♭ in A5 falls outside of the VII position and can easily be played by the 1st finger on the 6th fret of the 1st string.

At measure A11, you can again see the G major triad played against the Gmaj7 chord. In the following measure, the harmony is outlined by the G♯ of the E7 chord in the melody—very simple, but in this way you can really hear the harmony reflected in the melody we play.

Maintaining a Balance in the Duration of Notes

Lines of half notes give rise to eighth notes, which give rise to the quarter notes of measures A11–12. What you don't see here is endless eighth notes. When you have command of what you play, you can be rhythmically free and your playing will become more expressive.

Rhythmic Development

The étude starts out with melodies—played twice—composed of half notes that move naturally to new rhythmic material at A9, which then leads to new rhythmic material at A11, which leads to new rhythmic material at A13. The important thing is this: Each rhythm is developed and then leads you, in a natural way, to somewhere new.

Just for fun, let's see what would happen if we continued developing the rhythms in A9. Here's the original passage.

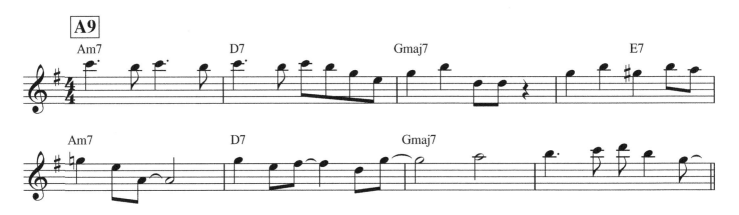

Here's one example of rhythmic development beginning at measure A9 . . .

TRACK 11

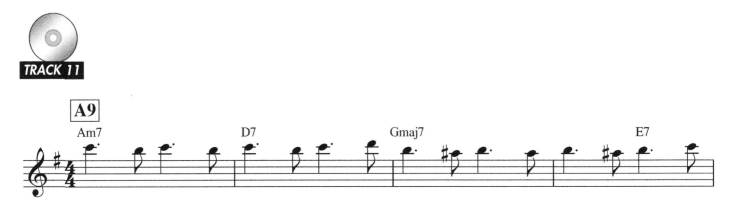

30

. . . and here's another.

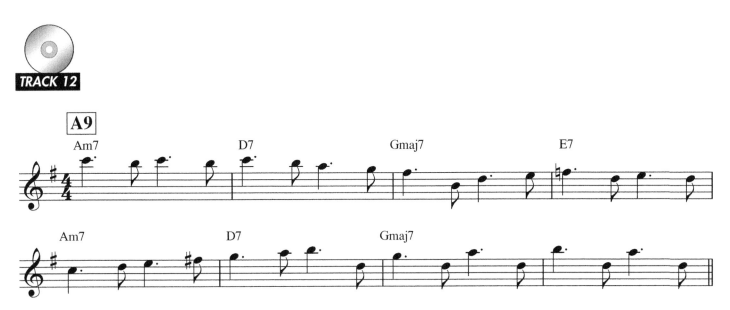

You should be able to develop and extend any rhythms you play. This will lead you naturally to new material—rhythmic and melodic—that you can then extend and develop again. In this way, you start your solos somewhere, those ideas lead somewhere else, and they lead somewhere else again. What you play has logic to it, and it is a lot like "telling a story." Now you're saying something!

In measures A19–21 below, the A♭ in the first measure falls outside the VII position and can be played by the 4th finger on the 11th fret of the 5th string, as opposed to the 10th fret—where the 4th finger would normally fall in the VII position. And since you've moved up one fret already, you can then play the F♯ at measure A20 with the 2nd finger, leading to the G at measure A21 being played at the 10th fret with the 4th finger. Now you're back in the normal VII position. This is a simple example of a more advanced approach to fingerings that will appear more and more frequently in the études to come.

At measure A40, reach out of the VII position to play the C♯ (at the 6th fret on the 3rd string) and slide to the D in its normal place in the VII position. Be careful, for even though we are sliding here, the listener should not be able to detect a slide, and should hear only the full and clear notes themselves.

ÉTUDE 6

TRACK 13

♩ = 118

B1

Chorus 2

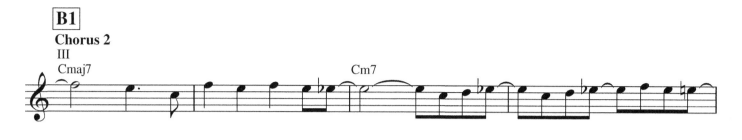

B9   **B10**

B11   **B14**

B17

B19

HANDS ON!

This étude enables you to play over the same song (in the same key) in two different positions. Chorus 1 is in the II position; Chorus 2 is in the III position.

At measure A9, we find the ii chord (Dm7) leading to the V chord (G7) at A10. Then, the raised 5th, a D♯, appears. The result is a triad composed of G–B–D♯: an *augmented triad*. Augmented tonalities are interesting. Let's think about them a bit more, OK? If we fill in the augmented triad by adding the steps that fall between the G–B–D♯ of the triad, we get the *augmented scale* (G–A–B–C♯–D♯–F–G), shown below.

This scale is composed entirely of *whole steps*. For this reason, the augmented scale is also frequently referred to as the *whole tone scale*. These are some interesting sounds, so let's take a closer look at some alternate ideas for this particular harmonic situation.

Here, very simply, we've added the F and proceeded up the scale in whole tones.

TRACK 14

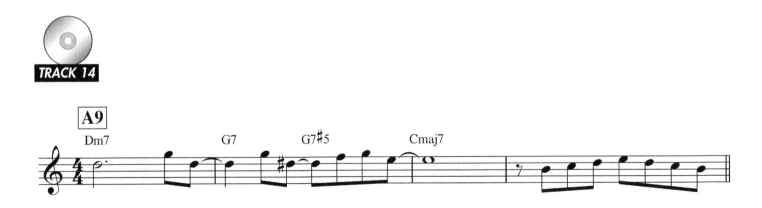

Here, we've followed the arpeggio down to the B, and then continued.

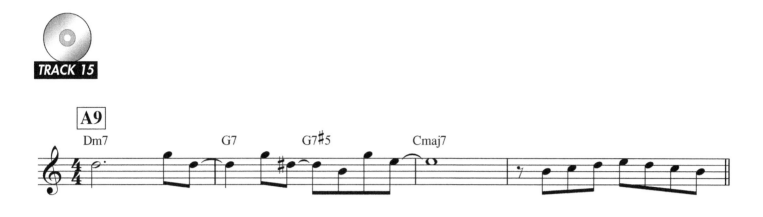

Now, let's try extending the augmented sound over the duration of A10 and see what we can come up with. This idea uses the notes of the augmented arpeggio.

Here's another idea using the notes of the augmented arpeggio.

Here's a more linear idea using the whole tone scale. Note the resolution (by half step) of the Ab to the G, the 5th of the Cmaj7 chord.

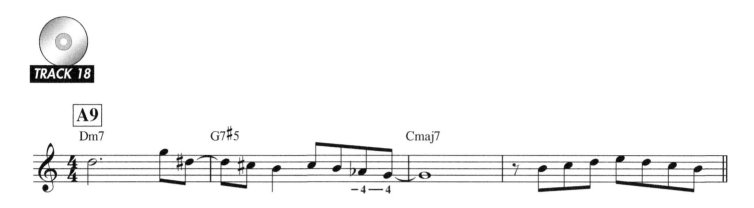

This one combines material from the augmented scale and the arpeggio.

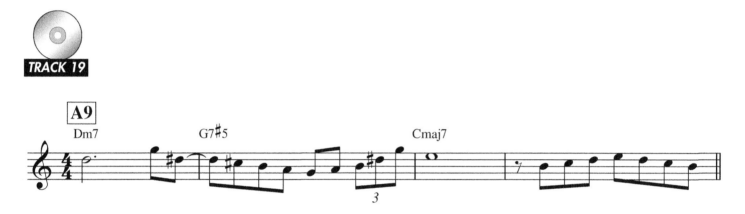

At B10 (which corresponds to the same place as the examples above, but in the following chorus) we find another G7♯5 chord. You might want to take a look at what takes place there with regard to the raised 5th, the augmented treatment it receives, and also how that material resolves to the Cmaj7 chord that follows. In any case, the important points are to be able to hear, recognize, and integrate augmented sounds into your playing to increase the range and dynamics of your melodic imagination.

At A32, the last measure of Chorus 1, you change positions. Once you've placed your 3rd finger one fret higher than it would normally play in the II position (on the C), all the other fingers fall right into place and you find yourself very easily moved up into the III position.

In measures B11–12, do you hear a little *quote* (a brief allusion to another song)? And then another at B17–19 (although altered in B19 to conform with the harmony at hand)?

At B14, there is yet another example of an easy way to make fingering simpler and more efficient. In this case, the 2nd finger isn't used where it normally would be in the III position, but so what? We have these flexible hands that can open and shut and be very clever at times. Why not bring the 2nd finger forward to play the D, leaving the 3rd finger free to play the C (as opposed to laying the 3rd finger down for both notes)? Play around with this alternative and see what you think!

ÉTUDE 7

TRACK 20

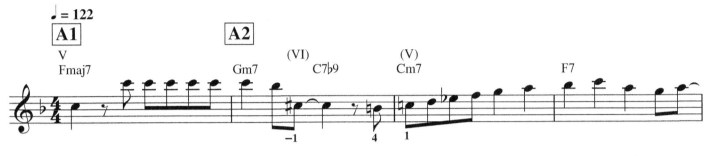

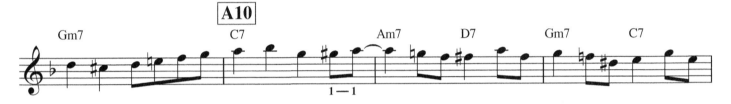

HANDS ON!

Étude 7 is roughly based on a structure called the "D. B. Blues" that was popularized by the great tenor saxophonist Lester Young. It consists of two blues choruses, followed by a bridge (a middle, or B section) based on a well-known chord progression, followed by another blues chorus. This is an *AABA form*—two roughly identical sections followed by something different, which is then, in turn, followed by another section roughly identical to the first and second. It's a wide-open canvas on which to paint.

Let's take a look at a few spots with regard to fingering, and the easy and very natural opening and closing of the hand that we do all the time.

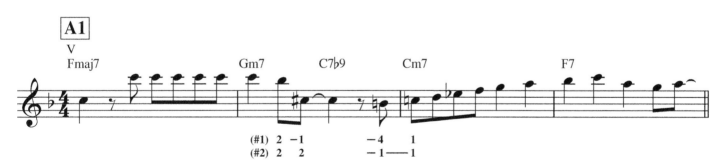

At A2, we can see the embodiment of the principle of using fingers that are available and free as first options. This is usually the most efficient and thus the easiest approach to fingering. What do I mean? Let's take a look and I'll try to explain.

Let's focus first on option #2, where you should play the notes exactly as they fall in the V position using the 2nd finger at the 6th fret on the 1st string to play the Bb, and then rock that same finger across two strings to play the C#. This would be followed by an opening of the hand to slide the 1st finger from the 4th to the 5th fret for the B♮ and C. The difficult part for many individuals is the rocking motion, and not the slide that follows.

Turning our attention now to option #1, play the C♯ at the 6th fret with the available and free 1st finger (one fret above where it usually falls in the V position), followed by the 4th finger for the B. When you open your hand and play the C with the 1st finger, you're back in the V position. Easy? Yes.

At A10, let's again look at two different approaches. Option #1 is simple: Open the hand to play the G♯ at the 4th fret, and then slide the 4th finger up a fret to play the A. Option #2 is less efficient and less workable at fast tempos: To go from the G to the G♯, you must force the 4th finger up a fret and then open the hand to play the A. I vote for #1.

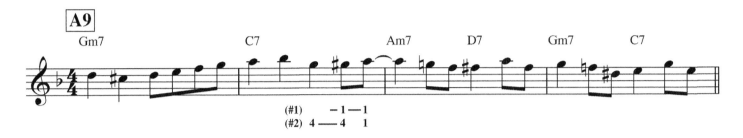

The fingering at A31 relates to what I wrote in regard to A10.

While option #2 is fine for many individuals, #1 is simple and avoids rocking across strings.

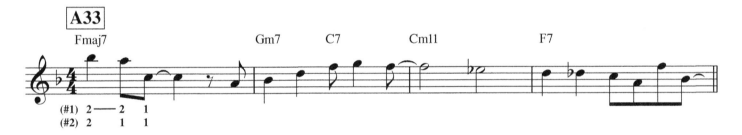

This one is simple! Open the hand to slide the 1st finger, and then open the hand to slide the 4th finger.

Simple again! Open the hand to play the G♭ and then slide the 4th finger back for the F.

How do you know when to slide fingers up, and when to slide fingers back? Is there anything you can use as a guide? Yes! It's the *chromatic scale*. If you haven't come across it before, take a look.

TRACK 21

Straight feel (no swing)

As the melody rises, you should open your hand and slide up with the 1st finger. As the melody descends, you should open your hand and slide back with the 4th finger. That's it. It's that simple.

Using these movements—opening the hand up and sliding up when a melody goes up, and opening up and sliding back when a melody descends—is applicable in more cases than not. Will this work 100 percent of the time? I'm afraid not, but it's a great general guide and approach.

The variations we come across in music are literally endless—no rule applies to every case. Never forget that the only answer for all of these questions of technique is in the music itself, the sound of what we play. If it sounds great, it *is* great. If not, we need to develop new techniques and approaches that allow us to express ourselves on our instruments, both musically and personally.

ÉTUDE 8

TRACK 22

HANDS ON!

In the *Simple Guide to Alternate Picking*, we focused first on quarter notes, and then predominantly on eighth notes. Remember, the essential principle of alternate picking is this: Your picking should at all times be in sync with the movement of your body. Thus, you play downstrokes on downbeats (the 1s, 2s, 3s, and 4s) and upstrokes on all of the upbeats (the "ands"). The guitar pick moves just the same way as your foot as it moves up and down to tap the beat.

But what happens in the instance of *triplets*, as they appear here at A15, A23, and A25?

One of the best features of alternate picking is that it's an approach to picking that always leaves your pick prepared for and ready to play (or *attack*) the next note. So let's allow that principle—that of having your pick prepared for the next attack—to be your guide with respect to developing an approach to playing triplets.

Let's focus on the triplet at A15. All three instances of triplets in *Étude 8* are similar in that they fall on down-beats, so the treatment in the other two instances is identical. Since the triplet starts on a downbeat—in this instance, on beat 4—you should start, as always, with a downstroke. There is nothing new here. For the second attack, the D, you should alternate (using an upstroke), and then alternate again for the third attack of the triplet, the F (a downstroke). Again, there is nothing new here. Continuing, we arrive at the first beat of A16, where you should feel your foot coming down on the downbeat (beat 1) and pick down, as usual. There's absolutely nothing new here either, and yet this is a place of possible confusion for many individuals.

Here are the two important things to keep in mind, both of which were touched upon in the section on alternate picking. First, it's important to develop the connection between your picking and the natural movement of your body. In that way, when "1" comes, you can't possibly miss—you know where it is, you feel it. Second, alternate picking does NOT mean mechanically alternating upstrokes and downstrokes—it means picking down on the downbeats and picking up on the upbeats. So, in the case of the last note of A15 and the first note of A16, it's no surprise that you should play them with two consecutive downstrokes.

How about taking a longer look at eighth note triplets? I have a feeling that you're up for it! Repeat the following lines until you are comfortable with them. They're all in the V position. Note that there's a pause between each line in the recording.

TRACK 23

Straight feel (no swing)

ÉTUDE 9

♩ = 116

A1

A5　　　　**A6**

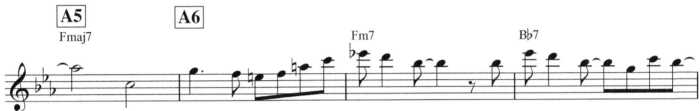

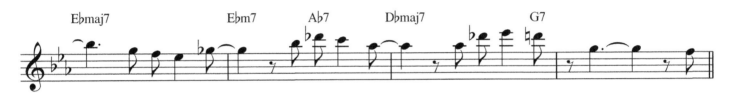

B1　　　　　　　　　**B3**

　　　　　　　　　　　　　　B8

B9

C1

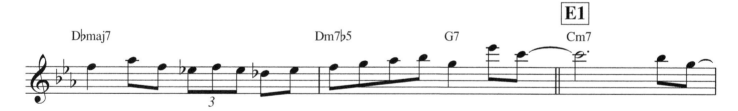

HANDS ON!

This is the simple alternative to using the 3rd finger to play the A and then rocking it over across two strings to play the C. This doesn't require much movement, so why not use the flexibility of our hands?

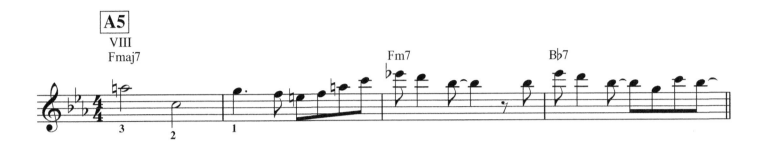

At B3 we run into two measures of practically nothing but attacks on upbeats! I love these off-the-beat rhythms, also known as *syncopations*.

There are two incidences of barring across two strings that are avoided by the very simple alternative fingering above. Take a look at what this passage would be like played with each finger where it would normally lie in the VIII position. Whoever wrote that line above about using the flexibility of our hands was a genius!

This is identical to the situation discussed above at A5.

At measure E1 we have a *coda*—or, simply put, an ending.

At E4 (3rd beat) and E6 (1st beat), there are two instances of the same rhythmic figure: a 16th note followed by a dotted eighth. To get a handle on this rhythm, you can think of it this way: It's as if you had two eighth notes, but took away half of the value of the first note (thus turning it into a 16th), and then added the value you took from the first note to the second (thus turning it into a dotted eighth). In both instances of this rhythm, the notes are the same—a G♭ moving down to an F (then to an E♭ and C). But what are these notes in terms of the harmony? The chords of the coda are no more than Cm7 moving to G7 and then back again to Cm7 (with a smattering of A♭7 and G7♯9) until the étude ends on an F13. In other words, for the entire coda, we are in the key of C minor, alternating between the i and the V chords of the key. And, looking even closer, the coda—a *vamp*, or repeated pattern—in C minor is composed essentially of these notes, which make up the C minor pentatonic scale.

Some rhythmic variations on this well-known scale are as follows.

TRACK 26

You've most likely have encountered this scale before. It's possible to invent endless variations and melodies (of which the coda of *Étude 9* is an example) with this simple, five-note scale.

There's frequently one more note added to the minor pentatonic scale that serves to make it sound even more bluesy. In fact, when you modify it this way, it's usually referred to as a *blues scale* instead of a minor pentatonic scale, and the added note—the ♭5— is called a *blue note*.

The G♭ at E4 and E6 comes from this scale.

Now, let's play around with different approaches to playing that 16th note–dotted eighth note figure that contains the G♭—the blue note. Of course, you can play it *straight*—that is, picked down and up (that's how it's notated in the étude). And this is how one would normally approach teaching this figure to beginners. But welcome to the real world! To get the most out of this bluesy, funky little thing, you need to *slur*. So let's do this.

TRACK 27

In slurring, you use the same fingers as you normally would to play both notes of the figure with the pick, but now only the first of the two notes is picked. To get enough volume on the second note (the F), you have to *pull off* slightly with your 4th finger when you play the first (the Gb)—the shorter of the two notes of the figure. Try it—it's nothing too difficult. Slurring is a device that, when applied to various situations, makes your playing more expressive. Keep this in mind: If your goal is to have your playing become as expressive and personal as possible, then you want everything you play to sound like it would if you were to sing it. That's what slurring does for your playing—it makes it more natural, more expressive, and sometimes, as in the figure we've been looking at here, even more funky and bluesy.

The coda, which, as was mentioned before, is essentially a vamp between the Cm7 and the G7 chords, has a surprise ending! The expectation is to hear another G7 just like all the others that came before, but instead it ends on an F13. Nice.

ÉTUDE 10

TRACK 28

♩ = 120

B1

Chorus 2

B15

B31

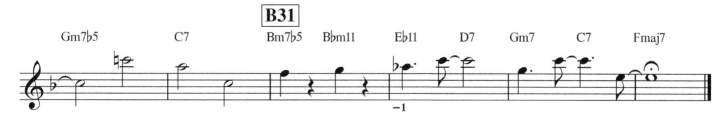

HANDS ON!

Étude 10 begins in the III position, but moves to the V position at A27. More positions, more fun! Right?

Is that a bit of a quote at B15? Or would thinking so be some sort of madness?

Since you've become such great readers by now and know about all there is to know about picking, why don't we jump all the way to B31 and take a look at the way this étude ends.

Do you remember the ending of *Étude 9*, where you vamped over the chords Cm7 and G7? And do you remember having read somewhere that, in my own view, the ending chord came as a surprise since the expectation was to hear yet another G7, just like the ones that had come before (rather than the F13 on which *Étude 9* does, in fact, finally end)? Believe it or not, the same kind of thing happens here.

In this case, you've played through two choruses of this song, and each time you've encountered a ii–V progression, it has lead to the tonic (as normally happens). But now, at the very end, when you're anticipating the final resolution to the tonic chord, the rug is pulled out from under you: It resolves not to the I chord (the Fmaj7 in this case), but moves instead to a Bm7♭5!

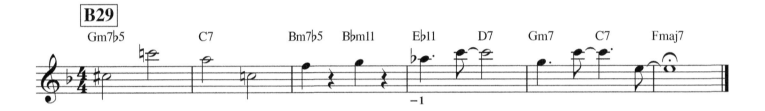

First off, this is not exactly an unknown ending. In fact, it has been played so frequently over the years that it has become somewhat of a cliché. But, aside from the fact that it's good to be aware of, it can serve us well in demonstrating the fact that there are virtually limitless possibilities when it comes to inventing melody. It also serves to demonstrate that we need to be aware of how to play basic chord forms and to be able to put whatever notes we want on top of those basic forms as melody. What do I mean? Read on. The most basic form of this ending is as follows.

Let me suggest some melody notes. In other words, play the chords that I've indicated, but use the melody notes I've written in below as the top notes (or melody notes) of the chords.

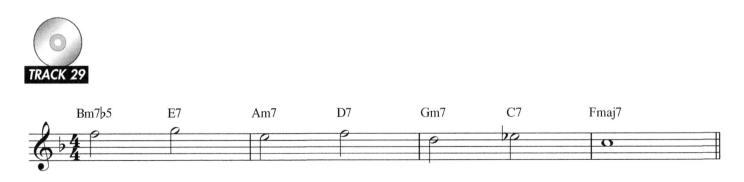

TRACK 29

Note that, in this melody, the top notes on the E7 chord, the D7 chord, and the C7 chord are all *tensions*— that is, notes other than chord tones. In each case, it's the ♯9. Can you play these chords using these melody notes? Work slowly through these chord sequences until you get them—chords *with* melody.

Here's another possibility.

This time I've changed the Am7 and Gm7 chords to m7♭5s to accommodate the chromatically descending melody line. Try playing slowly through this line—again, chords with melody.

Here's one more.

This melody jumps around. Try to follow it!

Now let's play around with the chords themselves a bit by making use of a few substitutions.

Here, the chords move down chromatically, but the melody stays on the F for the most part. Try experimenting with the sound by maintaining the F in the melody throughout.

Here's another idea, this time continuing the chromatic movement of the chords to the end.

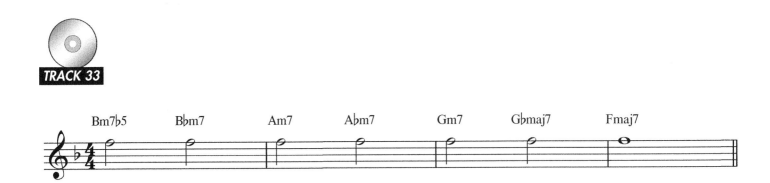

The point is this: Once you know your basic chord forms—and playing over these sorts of chord melodies is a great way to learn and practice them—you can use your melodic imagination to come up with nearly endless variations in terms of both melody and rhythm over this very simple ending.

Here are a few more that I hope might help stimulate some ideas of your own.

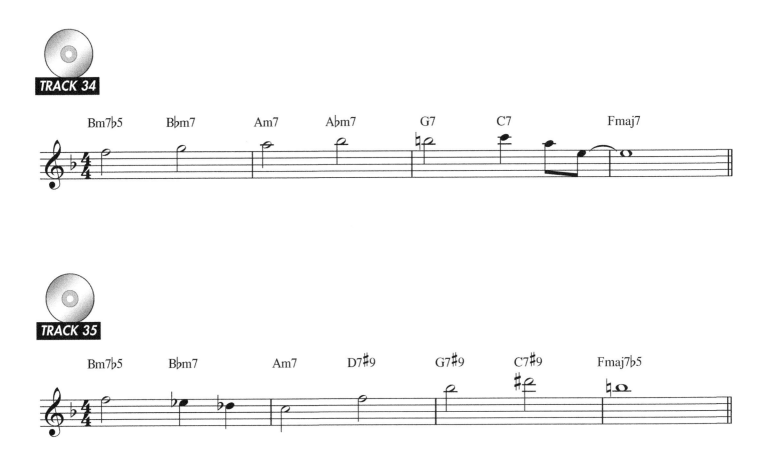

TRACK 36

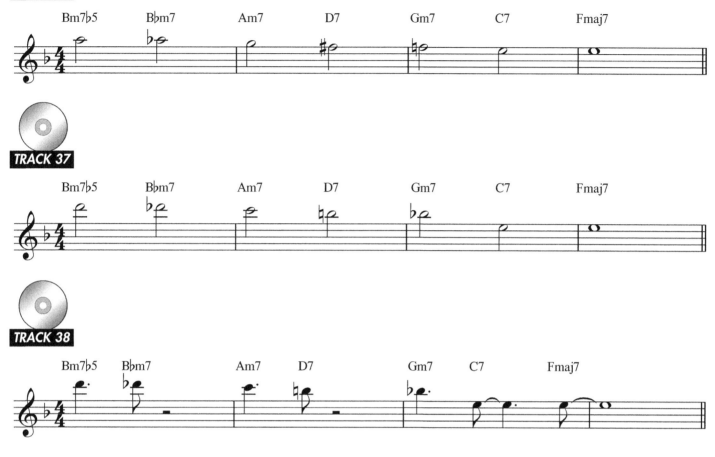

TRACK 37

TRACK 38

ÉTUDE 11

TRACK 39

♩ = 112

A1

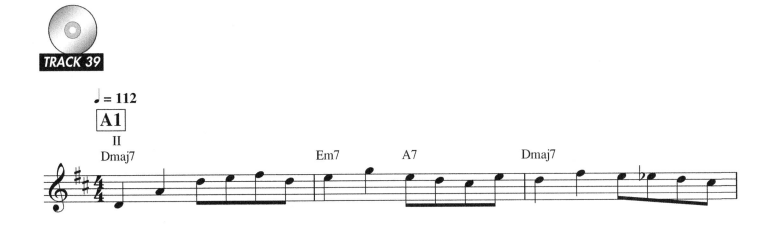

II
Dmaj7   Em7   A7   Dmaj7

Am7   D7   Gmaj7   G#°7

Dmaj7   B7   Em7

A7   Dmaj7   III   Fm7   Bb7

B1

Ebmaj7   Fm7   Bb7   Ebmaj7

Bbm7   Eb7   Abmaj7   A°7

Ebmaj7   C7   Fm7

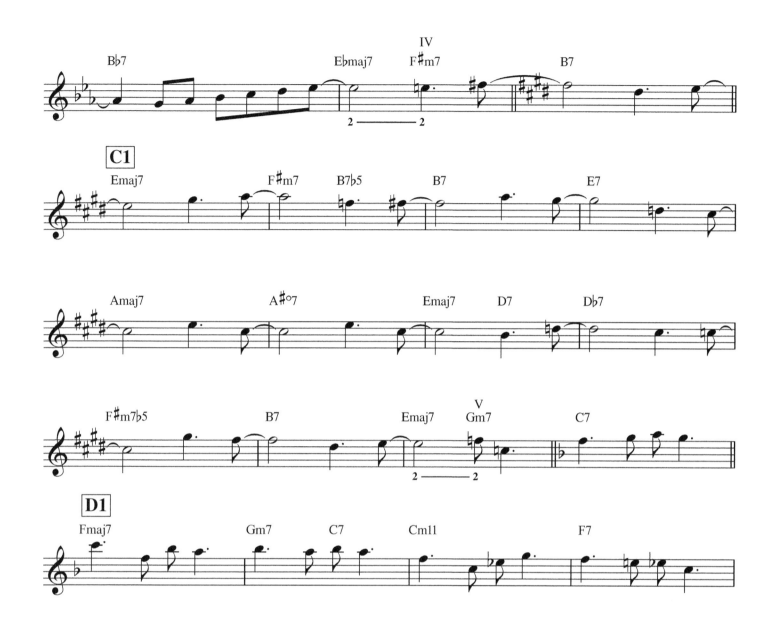

Étude 11 consists of four choruses of blues, starting in the key of D and ascending chromatically. Since you change positions with each change of key, you have practice here reading in all the positions from II through V.

Not only is this étude good for learning to read in multiple positions, it's an exercise in rhythmic development. Each chorus confines itself to the use of only one rhythm. And even though you wouldn't actually improvise chorus after chorus of blues—or of any other song, for that matter—using just one rhythm, to be able to do so is an excellent exercise and I recommend it to you. Why is the exercise of developing rhythms to the extreme valuable? Because being able to do so requires a mastery over what you play in both a melodic as well as a rhythmic sense. And that's one of our major goals as improvisers, isn't it: To be able to play whatever we want and to be able to do whatever we want with the material we play? To answer my own question: Yes, being able to play whatever we want and then to be able to do whatever we want with the things we play is one of our major goals. It's called *mastery* and it is one of the many aspects of developing your own voice and personality on your instrument.

Just for fun, let's fool around with Chorus 1 of *Étude 11*. Let's start by taking a look at an alternative chorus that uses the same rhythm as in the original.

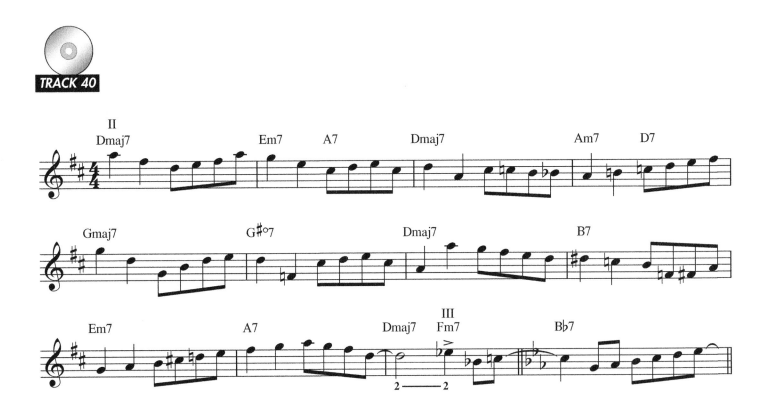

It's ironic that even though we're confined to just one rhythm, the possibilities are limitless.

Let's try rewriting Chorus 1, this time using a rhythm other than the original. You can pick anything—it doesn't really matter what rhythm you choose as long as you confine yourself to developing melodies over that rhythm only.

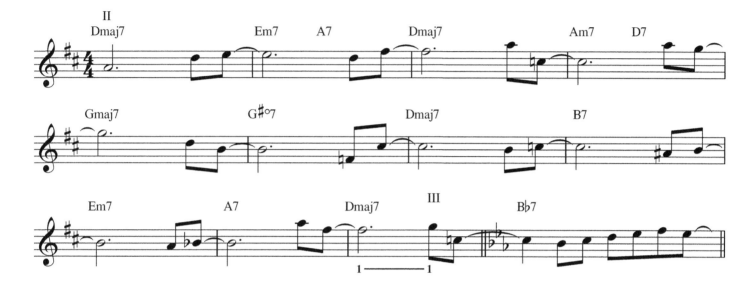

Try playing around with some of these improvising techniques yourself. If you like, you can write out your ideas at first, but you should develop the ability over time to come up with rhythms and melodies on your instrument without benefit of paper. Carry these abilities into the solos you improvise and see what happens. I guarantee that this will lead you to new and interesting places!

ÉTUDE 12

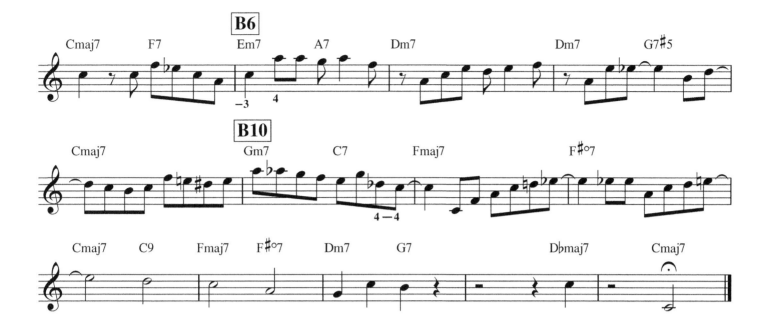

I don't know if I've left the best for last, but some of my students maintain that I may well have left the most *difficult* for last. Why is this the most difficult of the études? It's because of the picking and syncopation. There are also a few unusual spots with respect to fingering. When you can play smoothly through *Étude 12*, you'll be well on your way to having mastered the most important ideas we've been talking about and dealing with throughout the course of this book.

I won't go over the specifics with respect to the picking of A1 through A8 and beyond. You know how it works by now. Suffice it to note the large amount of *off-beat* attacks—attacks that fall on the "ands" of the beats—that need be picked with upstrokes.

At A10, open your hand to play the out-of-position G♯ on the 6th fret, and then slide back into position. There's nothing difficult or new here. You can refer back to our discussion of the chromatic scale in the commentary to *Étude 7* for an explanation of the reasoning behind this approach to fingering.

At A12–16, we have a quote from a well-known jazz blues. The original is by a colossus of a tenor saxophonist.

The concept behind the fingering at B6 has been touched on previously. Even though a fingering such as this is thought of as being rather advanced, it's really easy and goes a long way toward smoothing out otherwise more challenging passages.

Finally, at B10, open your hand to play the out-of-position D♭ on the 11th fret, and then slide back into position. As with the fingering at A10, there's nothing difficult or new here. As was true for A10, an explanation of the reason behind this approach to fingering is to be found in the commentary to *Étude 7* and the discussion of the chromatic scale.

My hope is that these etudes have helped you along in your understanding and mastery of improvisation and in your development into an artist who uses his improvisatory skills to express his own unique ideas and feelings. Keep your eyes on the prize, and happy picking!

A Simple Guide to Alternate Picking— Answers

Below are the rhythmic examples that appear beginning on pages 7–8, but with the counting and picking added. Repeat each of the following examples until the picking becomes clear and second nature.

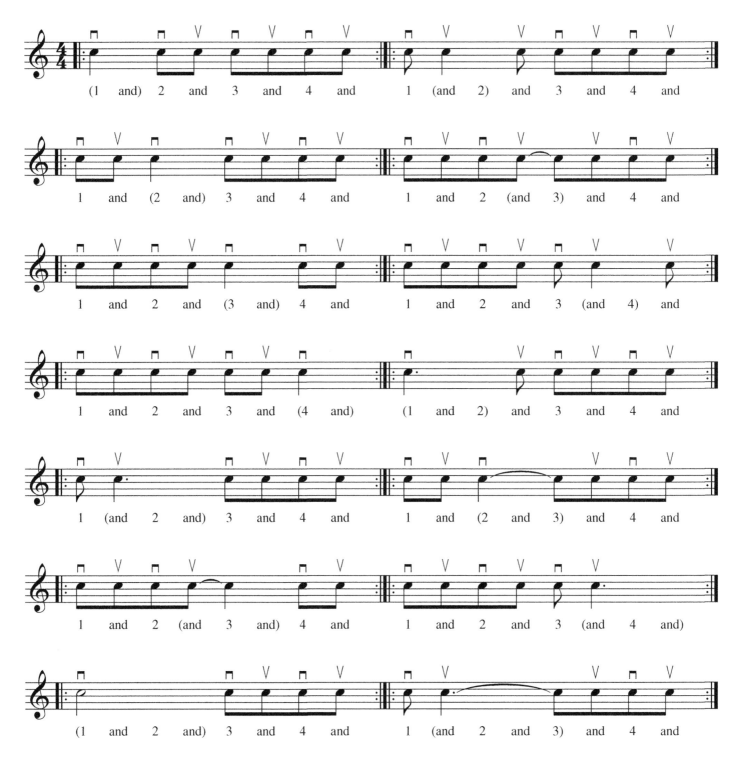